" i'm too young to be this d@*n old "

SOURCEBOOKS HYSTERIA™
AN IMPRINT OF SOURCEBOOKS, INC.®
NAPERVILLE, ILLINOIS

Published by Sourcebooks Hysteria, an imprint of Sourcebooks, Inc.
P.O. Box 4410, Naperville, Illinois 60567-4410
(630) 961-3900
FAX: (630) 961-2168
www.sourcebooks.com

Library of Congress Cataloging-in-Publication Data

I'm too young to be this d@*n old / [compiled by] Rachel Schwandt.
    p. cm.
  ISBN-13: 978-1-4022-0673-3
  ISBN-10: 1-4022-0673-9
  1. Age—Quotations, maxims, etc. 2. Aging—Quotations, maxims, etc. I.
Title: I am too young to be this d@*n old. II. Schwandt, Rachel.

  PN6084.A35I4 2006
  305.26—dc22
                              2005032126

Printed and bound in the United States of America
VP 10 9 8 7 6 5 4 3 2 1

" i'm too young
to be this d@*n old "

The advantage of having
a bad memory is that
you can enjoy the same
good things for the
first time several times.

                ❧ FRIEDRICH NIETZSCHE

Every time I think
that I am getting old,
and gradually going
to the grave,
something else happens.

❧ LILLIAN CARTER

We must always
have old memories and
young hopes.

❧ ARSÈNE HOUSSAYE

"I don't want ever to be a man," he said with passion. "I want always to be a little boy and to have fun."

❦ JAMES M. BARRIE, *PETER PAN*

The fact was I didn't want to look my age, but I didn't want to act the age I wanted to look either. I also wanted to grow old enough to understand that sentence.

❦ ERMA BOMBECK

People who say
you're just as old as
you feel are all wrong,
fortunately.

 RUSSELL BAKER

We have a lot to do…People don't understand this. They think we're sitting around in rocking chairs, which isn't at all true. Why, we don't even own a rocking chair.

The young may know
the rules, but we know
the exceptions.

History will be
kind to me,
for I intend to write it.

❧ WINSTON CHURCHILL

The principal objection
to old age is that there's
no future in it.

❧ Anonymous

"

If I'd known I was
gonna live this long,
I'd have taken better
care of myself.

❦ EUBIE BLAKE

If you don't want to
get old,
don't mellow.

☙ LINDA ELLERBEE

Let me advise thee not
to talk of thyself as being
old....if thee continually
talks of thyself as being
old, thee may perhaps
bring on some of the
infirmities of age.
At least I would not risk
it if I were thee.

❧ HANNAH WHITALL SMITH

Forty is the old age
of youth. Fifty is the
youth of old age.

                   ❧ FRENCH PROVERB

All the humiliating, tragicomic, heartbreaking things happened to me in my girlhood, and nothing makes me happier than to realize I cannot possibly relive my youth.

❦ ILKA CHASE

Experience enables you to recognize a mistake when you make it again.

❦ FRANKLIN P. JONES

"

When you get to be
my age, all your friends
have either died or
moved to Florida.

        ❧ HELEN VAN SLYKE

A proverb is a
short sentence based on
long experience.

              ❦ MIGUEL DE CERVANTES

I'm saving that rocker
for the day when I feel
as old as I really am.

❧ Dwight D. Eisenhower

Middle age is when
your narrow waist and
broad mind begin to
change places.

A life spent in making mistakes is not only more honorable but more useful than a life spent doing nothing.

ঽ GEORGE BERNARD SHAW

Nobody knows the age of the human race, but all agree that it is old enough to know better.

In spite of the cost of living, it's still popular.

❧ KATHLEEN NORRIS

Let us endeavor to live
so that when we die
even the undertaker will
be sorry.

        ❧ MARK TWAIN

The years between fifty and seventy are the hardest. You are always being asked to do things, and yet you are not decrepit enough to turn them down.

❦ T.S. ELIOT

Seal my lips on aches and pains. They are increasing, and love of rehearsing them is becoming sweeter as the years go by.

❧ ROSALIND RUSSELL

I may not be
totally perfect, but
parts of me are excellent.

❧ ASHLEIGH BRILLIANT

I'm at an age when
my back goes out more
than I do.

ꙮ PHYLLIS DILLER

"

You know you are
getting old when
the gleam in your eyes
is from the sun hitting
your bifocals.

I have made mistakes,
but I have never made
the mistake of claiming
that I never made one.

❧ JAMES GORDON BENNETT

Be wiser than other
people, if you can;
but do not tell them so.

❧ LORD CHESTERFIELD

I never deny,
I never contradict.
I sometimes forget.

❧ BENJAMIN DISRAELI

I was born in the wrong generation. When I was a young man, no one had any respect for youth. Now I am an old man and no one has any respect for age.

‡ BERTRAND RUSSELL

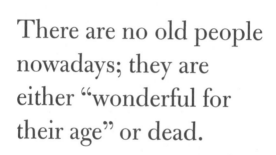

There are no old people nowadays; they are either "wonderful for their age" or dead.

❧ Mary Pettibone Poole

Half our life is spent trying to find something to do with the time we have rushed through life trying to save.

❧ WILL ROGERS

It is not a sin to be
seventy, but it is also
no joke.

❧ GOLDA MEIR

The worst waste of breath, next to playing the saxophone, is advising a son.

♦ FRANK MCKINNEY

I want to have children while my parents are still young enough to take care of them.

❧ RITA RUDNER

I don't plan to grow old
gracefully. I plan to
have face-lifts until
my ears meet.

❧ RITA RUDNER

I've got everything
I always had. Only it's
six inches lower.

 ℰ Gypsy Rose Lee

41

My grandmother's ninety. She's dating. He's ninety-three. It's going great. They never argue. They can't hear each other.

※ CATHY LADMAN

I don't understand when people say a lover is "too old" or "too young."
As far as I'm concerned, *anyone* who is on the planet the same time you are is fair game.

❧ FLASH ROSENBERG

I am luminous with age.

 ❧ MERIDEL LE SUEUR

She had accomplished what according to builders is only possible to wood and stone of the very finest grain; she had *weathered,* as they call it, with beauty.

Though drab outside—
wreckage to the eye,
mirrors a mortification—
inside we flame with a
wild life that is almost
incommunicable.

❧ Florida Scott-Maxwell

An old earthen pipe like myself is dry and thirsty and so a most voracious drinker of life at its source; I'm no more to be split by the vital stream than if I were stone or steel.

 ELINOR WYLIE

Life is short, but it's wide.

              ❦ SPANISH PROVERB

The great thing about
getting older is that
you don't lose all the
other ages you've been.

❧ MADELEINE L'ENGLE

The dying process
begins the minute we are
born, but it accelerates
during dinner parties.

❧ CAROL MATTHAU

My grandmother was a very tough woman. She buried three husbands. Two of them were just napping.

❦ RITA RUDNER

My grandmother started
walking five miles a day
when she was sixty.
She's ninety-seven today
and we don't know
where the hell she is.

❧ ELLEN DEGENERES

Quite useless to discuss
questions of age with old
people, they have such
peculiar ideas on the
subject. "Not really old
at all, only seventy,"
you hear them saying.

❧ NANCY MITFORD

Man fools himself.
He prays for a long life,
and he fears old age.

❧ CHINESE PROVERB

Middle age—later than you think and sooner than you expect.

❦ EARL WILSON

Of middle age the best that can be said is that a middle-aged person has likely learned how to have a little fun in spite of his troubles.

 🚀 DON MARQUIS

The best things in life
are free, but it costs a lot
of time and money
before you find this out.

Experience is the name
everyone gives to
his mistakes.

              ❧ OSCAR WILDE

By the time the youngest
children have learned to
keep the place tidy,
the oldest grandchildren
are on hand to
tear it to pieces again.

❧ CHRISTOPHER MORLEY

You don't stop laughing
because you grow old;
you grow old because
you stop laughing.

❧ MICHAEL PRITCHARD

[Middle age] occurs when you are too young to take up golf and when you are too old to rush up to the net.

❧ FRANKLIN P. ADAMS

Most people say that as you get old, you have to give up things. I think you get old *because* you give up things.

❧ SENATOR THEODORE F. GREEN

Before undergoing a surgical operation, arrange your temporal affairs. You may live.

❦ AMBROSE BIERCE

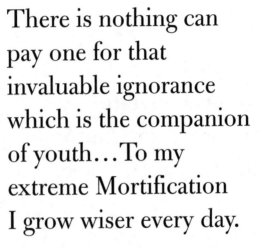

There is nothing can
pay one for that
invaluable ignorance
which is the companion
of youth…To my
extreme Mortification
I grow wiser every day.

❦ LADY MARY WORTLEY MONTAGU

Before I got married
I had six theories about
bringing up children;
now I have six children
and no theories.

❧ JOHN WILMOT, EARL OF ROCHESTER

The trouble with using experience as a teacher is that the final exam often comes first and the lesson second.

If a man has come to that point where he is so content that he says, "I do not want to know any more, or do any more, or be any more," he is in a state of which he ought to be changed into a mummy.

❧ HENRY WARD BEECHER

Twenty years from now you will be more disappointed by the things you didn't do than by the ones you did do. So throw off the bowlines. Sail away from the safe harbor. Catch the trade winds in your sails. Explore. Dream. Discover.

❧ MARK TWAIN

It takes a long time
to grow young.

☙ PABLO PICASSO

The first forty years of life give us the text; the next thirty supply the commentary on it.

❧ ARTHUR SCHOPENHAUER

There is something about the present which we would not exchange, though we were offered a choice of all past ages to live in.

❧ VIRGINIA WOOLF

We don't understand life
any better at forty than
at twenty, but we know it
and admit it.

⚬ JULES RENARD

The man who is too old
to learn was probably
always too old to learn.

❦ HENRY S. HASKINS

It is never too late to
give up our prejudices.

❧ HENRY DAVID THOREAU

My comfort is, that old age, that ill layer-up of beauty, can do no more spoil upon my face.

❦ WILLIAM SHAKESPEARE

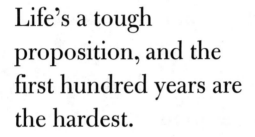

Life's a tough proposition, and the first hundred years are the hardest.

❧ WILSON MIZNER

It's all that the young can do for the old, to shock them and keep them up to date.

❦ GEORGE BERNARD SHAW

There's many a good
tune played on an old
fiddle.

❧ SAMUEL BUTLER

Her grandmother, as she gets older, is not fading but rather becoming more concentrated.

❧ PAULETTE BATES ALDEN

It is sad to grow old but nice to ripen.

❦ BRIGITTE BARDOT

Cheerfulness and contentment are great beautifiers and are famous preservers of youthful looks.

❧ CHARLES DICKENS

I speak the truth, not my fill of it, but as much as I dare speak; and I dare to do so a little more as I grow old.

& MICHEL DE MONTAIGNE

Youth is happy because it has the ability to see beauty. Anyone who keeps the ability to see beauty never grows old.

❧ FRANZ KAFKA

Being young is beautiful,
but being old
is comfortable.

☙ MARIE VON EBNER-ESCHENBACH

Always be nice to those younger than you, because they are the ones who will be writing about you.

❦ CYRIL CONNOLLY

It was formerly a
terrifying view to me
that I should one day be
an old woman. I now
find that Nature has
provided pleasures for
every state.

❧ LADY MARY WORTLEY MONTAGU

Age does not protect you from love. But love, to some extent, protects you from age.

❧ JEANNE MOREAU

People are constantly warned not to overdo. It is only by overdoing sometimes that we learn how much we *can* do.

֍ MARJORIE BARSTOW GREENBIE

I'm sixty-five, and I
guess that puts me in
with the geriatrics; but if
there were fifteen
months in every year,
I'd only be forty-eight.

❧ JAMES THURBER

"

My mother used to say:
The older you get, the
better you get—unless
you're a banana.

❧ ROSE, *THE GOLDEN GIRLS*

The secret of staying young is to live honestly, eat slowly, and lie about your age.

❧ LUCILLE BALL

I'd like to grow very old
as slowly as possible.

❦ IRENE MAYER SELZNICK

Do not deprive me
of my age.
I've earned it.

☙ MAY SARTON

The hardest years in life
are those between ten
and seventy.

❦ HELEN HAYES (AT 73)

Your life story would not
make a good book.
Don't even try.

❧ FRAN LEBOWITZ

Anybody who thinks they know everything ain't been around long enough to know anything.

❧ GLADIOLA MONTANA

I try to take one day at a time, but sometimes several days attack me at once.

❧ JENNIFER UNLIMITED

There are days of oldness, and then one gets young again. It goes backward and forward, not in one direction.

❧ KATHARINE BUTLER HATHAWAY

Inside every older person is a younger person wondering what happened.

⟡ JENNIFER UNLIMITED

I have a problem about being nearly sixty: I keep waking up in the morning and thinking I'm thirty-one.

❦ ELIZABETH JANEWAY

I haven't known what to
do for so long,
I'm getting good at it.

& FLASH ROSENBERG

Life is something to do
when you can't get
to sleep.

❧ FRAN LEBOWITZ

If I had my past life over again, I'd make all the same mistakes—only sooner.

❧ TALLULAH BANKHEAD

They say the movies
should be more like life.
I think life should be
more like the movies.

❦ MYRNA LOY

It's not true that life is one damn thing after another—it's one damn thing over and over.

❦ EDNA ST. VINCENT MILLAY

If you can't be a good example, then you'll just have to be a horrible warning.

✎ CATHERINE AIRD

In August, my husband and I celebrated our thirty-eighth wedding anniversary. You know what I finally realized? If I had killed that man the first time I thought about it, I'd have been out of jail by now.

❧ ANITA MILNER

"

I'm thirty-three, single…Don't you think it's a generalization you should be married at thirty-three? That's like looking at somebody who's seventy and saying, "Hey, when are you gonna break your hip? All your friends are breaking their hips—what are you waiting for?"

❧ SUE KOLINSKY

To George Burns:
George, you're too old to get married again. Not only can't you cut the mustard, honey, you're too old to open the jar.

❧ LA WANDA PAGE

Getting old
ain't for sissies.

❧ BETTE DAVIS

I don't know how you
feel about old age…but
in my case I didn't
even see it coming.
It hit me from the rear.

❧ PHYLLIS DILLER

Thirty-five is when you finally get your head together and your body starts falling apart.

❧ CARYN LESCHEN

Don't think of it as wrinkles. Think of it as relaxed-fit skin.

❦ CATHY CRIMMINS

The good thing about going to your twenty-five-year high school reunion is that you get to see all your old classmates. The bad thing is that they get to see you.

❦ ANITA MILNER

You can't stay young forever, but you can be immature for the rest of your life.

❧ MAXINE WILKIE

The older one grows,
the more one likes
indecency.

                ❦ VIRGINIA WOOLF

The older I get,
the simpler the definition
of maturity seems:
it's the length of time
between when I realize
someone is a jackass and
when I tell them that
they're one.

❧ BRETT BUTLER

Don't get upset about wrinkles: they're just foreshadowing.

❦ CATHY CRIMMINS

A woman came to ask the doctor if a woman should have children after thirty-five. I said thirty-five is enough for any woman!

❦ GRACIE ALLEN

Age is something that
doesn't matter, unless
you are a cheese.

      ❧ BILLIE BURKE

I'm at an age where I think more about food than sex. Last week I put a mirror over my dining room table.

❧ RODNEY DANGERFIELD

From birth to age
eighteen, a girl needs
good parents, from
eighteen to thirty-five she
needs good looks, from
thirty-five to fifty-five she
needs a good personality,
and from fifty-five on she
needs cash.

❦ SOPHIE TUCKER

Another belief of mine: that everyone else my age is an adult, whereas I am merely in disguise.

❧ MARGARET ATWOOD

66

If this was adulthood,
the only improvement
she could detect in her
situation was that now
she could eat dessert
without eating her
vegetables.

❧ LISA ALTHER

It is better to wear out
than to rust out.

❧ RICHARD CUMBERLAND

Maybe I'm an adult because my friends are. Could that be the way you tell? My friends are tall and drink coffee and have sex.

❧ ADAIR LARA

The lovely thing about being forty is that you can appreciate twenty-five-year-old men more.

❦ COLLEEN MCCULLOUGH

Maybe no one actually turns into an adult. Maybe you just get to be an older and older kid. Maybe the whole world is being run by old kids.

❦ ADAIR LARA

Experience: A comb life gives you after you lose your hair.

❦ JUDITH STERN

Eighty's a landmark and people treat you differently than they do when you're seventy-nine. At seventy-nine, if you drop something it just lies there. At eighty, people pick it up for you.

❦ HELEN VAN SLYKE

Living in the past is a dull and lonely business; looking back strains the neck muscles, causes you to bump into people not going your way.

❦ EDNA FERBER

The older I get, the
faster I was.

❧ UNKNOWN

It's nice to be here.
When you're ninety-nine
years old, it's nice to be
anyplace.

❧ GEORGE BURNS

Eighty years old! No eyes left, no ears, no teeth, no legs, no wind! And when all is said and done, how astonishingly well one does without them!

       ❧ PAUL CLAUDEL

I must be getting old…People are beginning to tell me I *look so young*.

❧ L.M. MONTGOMERY

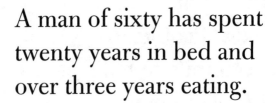

A man of sixty has spent twenty years in bed and over three years eating.

❦ ARNOLD BENNETT

You will recognize my boy, the first sign of old age: It is when you go out into the streets of London and realize for the first time how young the policemen look.

❧ SIR SEYMOUR HICKS

You know you're getting old when the candles cost more than the cake.

❦ BOB HOPE

Old people are fond of giving good advice; it consoles them for no longer being capable of setting a bad example.

❦ FRANÇOIS DE LA ROCHEFOUCAULD

Age is mind over matter.
If you don't mind, it
doesn't matter.

❧ LEROY "SATCHEL" PAIGE

The whiter my hair
becomes, the more ready
people are to believe
what I say.

❧ BERTRAND RUSSELL

All of a sudden, I'm older than my parents were when I thought *they* were old.

    ❦ LOIS WYSE

It's a sign of age if you
feel like the morning
after the night before
and you haven't been
anywhere.

ℰ ANONYMOUS

Old age is a great trial,
John. One has to be so
damned *good!*

☙ MAY SARTON

Never allow your child
to call you by your first
name. He hasn't known
you long enough.

❦ FRAN LEBOWITZ

It's hard to feel middle-aged, because how can you tell how long you are going to live?

♪ MIGNON MCLAUGHLIN

Middle age is when you get in the car and immediately change the radio station.

❧ PATRICIA PENTON LEIMBACH

I've always believed in
the adage that the secret
of eternal youth is
arrested development.

❦ ALICE ROOSEVELT LONGWORTH

I don't want to achieve
immortality through my
work…I want to achieve
it through not dying.

             ❦ WOODY ALLEN

"

Life is to be lived. If you
have to support yourself,
you had bloody well
better find some way that
is going to be interesting.
And you don't do that by
sitting around wondering
about yourself.

        ❧ KATHARINE HEPBURN

Some people die at twenty-five and aren't buried until they are seventy-five.

 BENJAMIN FRANKLIN

We cannot be *normal* and *alive* at the same time.

❦ E.M. CIORAN

There's got to be more to life than sittin' here watchin' *Days of Our Lives* and foldin' your Fruit of the Looms.

❦ Mama, *Mama's Family*

It seems necessary to completely shed the old skin before the new, brighter, stronger, more beautiful one can emerge…I never thought I'd be getting a life lesson from a snake!

☙ JULIE RIDGE

Sometimes I would
almost rather have
people take away years
of my life than take away
a moment.

❧ PEARL BAILEY

Middle age is when you find out where the action is so you can go someplace else.

❧ PATRICIA PENTON LEIMBACH

And then, not expecting it, you become middle-aged and anonymous. No one notices you. You achieve a wonderful freedom. It is a positive thing. You can move about, unnoticed and invisible.

❦ DORIS LESSING

You grow up the day
you have your first real
laugh at yourself.

❦ ETHEL BARRYMORE

Everything else you grow out of, but you never recover from childhood.

❦ BERYL BAINBRIDGE

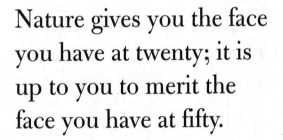

Nature gives you the face
you have at twenty; it is
up to you to merit the
face you have at fifty.

৬ COCO CHANEL

After a certain number of years our faces become our biographies.

                         ❧ CYNTHIA OZICK

I've always roared with laughter when they say life begins at forty....The day I was born was when life began for me.

❧ BETTE DAVIS

It is never too late—
in fiction or in life—
to revise.

❧ NANCY THAYER

If we could sell our experiences for what they cost us we'd be millionaires.

❧ ABIGAIL VAN BUREN

I have a simple philosophy. Fill what's empty. Empty what's full. And scratch where it itches.

 ALICE ROOSEVELT LONGWORTH

Vitality! That's the
pursuit of life, isn't it?

❦ KATHARINE HEPBURN

I might repeat to myself, slowly and soothingly, a list of quotations beautiful from minds profound; if I can remember any of the damn things.

❦ DOROTHY PARKER

"

While others may argue about whether the world ends with a bang or a whimper, I just want to make sure mine doesn't end with a whine.

❧ BARBARA GORDON

Life itself is the proper binge.

❧ Julia Child

Time wounds all heels.

❦ JANE ACE

One learns in life to keep silent and draw one's own confusions.

❧ CORNELIA OTIS SKINNER

I think the one lesson I have learned is that there is no substitute for paying attention.

❧ DIANE SAWYER

Someone said that life is a party. You join in after it's started and leave before it's finished.

❦ ELSA MAXWELL

If only we'd stop trying to be happy, we could have a pretty good time.

❧ EDITH WHARTON

The older I get, the greater power I seem to have to help the world; I am like a snowball— the further I am rolled, the more I gain.

❧ SUSAN B. ANTHONY

One part of him is old
and another is still
unborn.

❧ ELIAS CANETTI

I am old enough to tell the truth. It is one of the privileges of age.

 GEORGES CLEMENCEAU

After the age of eighty,
all contemporaries are
friends.

❦ MADAME DE DINO

"

It is nonsense for you to talk of old age so long as you outrun young men in the race for service and in the midst of anxious times fill rooms with your laughter and inspire youth with hope when they are on the brink of despair.

ॐ MOHANDAS GANDHI

"

"

I'm now at the age
where I've got to prove
that I'm just as good as I
never was.

❦ REX HARRISON

Oh to be seventy again.

❦ OLIVER WENDELL HOLMES, JR. *UPON*
SEEING AN ATTRACTIVE WOMAN ON HIS
NINETIETH BIRTHDAY.

How old would you be if you didn't know how old you were?

❦ LEROY "SATCHEL" PAIGE

Most people are dead at
my age anyway. You
could look it up.

❧ CASEY STENGEL

In youth we run into difficulties, in old age, difficulties run into us.

❧ JOSH BILLINGS

Old Boys have their
Playthings as well as
young Ones;
the Difference is only in
the Price.

❧ BENJAMIN FRANKLIN, *POOR RICHARD'S
ALMANACK*

Whereas in my youth I succeeded daily and under all circumstances, I now succeed only periodically and under favorable conditions.

❦ GOETHE

If a young or middle-aged man, when leaving a company, does not recollect where he has laid his hat, it is nothing; but if the same inattention is discovered in an old man, people will shrug up their shoulders, and say, "His memory is going."

❦ SAMUEL JOHNSON

From the earliest times
the old have rubbed it
into the young that they
are wiser than they, and
before the young had
discovered what nonsense
this was they were old
too, and it profited them
to carry on the imposture.

❧ W. Somerset Maugham

It's true, some wines improve with age. But only if the grapes were good in the first place.

❦ ABIGAIL VAN BUREN

I will not make age an issue…I am not going to exploit for political purposes my opponent's youth and inexperience.

❧ RONALD REAGAN

Falstaff: A man can no more separate age and covetousness than 'a can part young limbs and lechery.

❦ SHAKESPEARE, *HENRY IV*

The denunciation of the young is a necessary part of the hygiene of older people and greatly assists the circulation of their blood.

❧ Logan Pearsall Smith

I am not young enough
to know everything.

❧ J.M. BARRIE

Young men are as apt to think themselves wise enough, as drunken men are to think themselves sober enough.

§ LORD CHESTERFIELD

The young always have the same problem—how to rebel and conform at the same time. They have now solved this by defying their parents and copying one another.

❧ QUENTIN CRISP

Youth is a wonderful thing. What a crime to waste it on children.

☙ GEORGE BERNARD SHAW

What is more enchanting
than the voices of young
people, when you can't
hear what they say?

❦ LOGAN PEARSALL SMITH

It's not that I'm afraid to die. I just don't want to be there when it happens.

❦ WOODY ALLEN

We die only once, and
it's for such a long time!

            ❧ MOLIÈRE

199

I don't mind having to die. I've had my good time…and I don't mind having to pay for it. But to think that those swine will say that I'm out of the game.

❦ THEODORE ROOSEVELT

No one is so old as to think he cannot live one more year.

❧ CICERO

The best way to ensure a
long, productive life is to
have a chronic disease
and take care of it.

❧ OLIVER WENDELL HOLMES

I'm a 101 years old and at my age, honey, I can say what I want!

❧ Bessie Delany

The idea is to die young
as late as possible.

❦ ASHLEY MONTAGU

A Lacedaemonian was asked what had made him live healthy so long. "Ignorance of medicine," he replied.

❦ MONTAIGNE

What have I done to achieve longevity? Woken up each morning and tried to remember not to wear my hearing aid in the bath.

It isn't time to die yet. I am needed by my children and grandchildren, and it isn't bad in this world—except that I can't turn the earth over, and it has become difficult to climb trees.

꙰ AKHBA SULEIMAN (AGE 99)

I am forty years old now, and forty years, after all is a whole lifetime; after all, that is extremely old age. To live longer than forty years is bad manners; it is vulgar, immoral.

❧ Fyodor Dostoyevsky

Boys'll be boys, an' so'll a lot o' middle-aged men.

⚬ KIN HUBBARD

> I have been to a ball at Weimar. The Emperor Alexander dances, but I don't. Forty is forty.

❧ NAPOLEON (IN A LETTER TO JOSEPHINE)

Middle age is when it takes longer to rest than to get tired.

❦ LAURENCE J. PETER

It isn't so astonishing, the number of things that I can remember, as the number of things I can remember that aren't so.

⌀ JOSH BILLINGS

I remember things the way they should have been.

          ❧ TRUMAN CAPOTE

I sometimes worry about my short attention span, but not for very long.

ℰ STRANGE DE JIM

"

I like to think of my behavior in the sixties as a "learning experience." Then again, I like to think of anything stupid I've done as a "learning experience." It makes me feel less stupid.

❧ P.J. O'Rourke

We learn from experience that men never learn anything from experience.

❦ GEORGE BERNARD SHAW

The greater part of what my neighbors call good I believe in my soul to be bad, and if I repent of anything, it is very likely to be my good behavior. What demon possessed me that I behaved so well?

❧ HENRY DAVID THOREAU

I love to see a young girl
go out and grab the
world by the lapels.
Life's a bitch. You've got
to go out and kick ass.

❧ MAYA ANGELOU

To live is like to love—all reason is against it, and all healthy instinct for it.

❧ SAMUEL BUTLER

I believe in life after birth.

 ❖ MAXIE DUNHAM

At fifty the madwoman
in the attic breaks loose,
stomps down the stairs,
and sets fire to the
house. She won't be
imprisoned anymore.

❧ ERICA JONG

Do not take life too
seriously—you will
never get out of it alive.

❧ ELBERT HUBBARD

Life is one day at a time. And thank God! I couldn't take much more.

❧ Daniel Patrick Moynihan

If I wanted life to be easy, I should have gotten born in a different universe.

ℰ Rebecca West

Life does not cease to be funny when people die any more than it ceases to be serious when people laugh.

 George Bernard Shaw

Death and taxes and childbirth! There's never any convenient time for any of them.

⚬ SCARLETT O'HARA

Die, my dear doctor! That's the last thing I shall do!

🖎 HENRY JOHN TEMPLE, LORD PALMERSTON

Death is just nature's way
of telling you, "Hey,
you're not alive anymore."

    ❧ Bull, *Night Court*

Death is a low chemical trick played on everybody except sequoia trees.

❧ J.J. FURNAS

When you don't have
any money, the problem
is food. When you have
money it's sex. When
you have both it's
health. If everything is
simply jake, then you're
frightened of death.

❧ J.P. DONLEAVY

When you're my age,
you just never risk being
ill—because then
everyone says: "Oh,
he's done for."

❧ Sir John Gielgud

" I have always felt that a woman has the right to treat the subject of her age with ambiguity until, perhaps, she passes into the realm of over ninety. Then it is better that she be candid with herself and with the world.

❧ HELENA RUBINSTEIN

"

Never trust a woman
who will not lie about
her age after thirty. She
is unwomanly and
unhuman and there is no
knowing what crimes
she will commit.

❧ GERTRUDE ATHERTON

The years that a woman subtracts from her age are not lost: they are added to the ages of other women.

& DIANE DE POITIERS

I refuse to admit that I am more than fifty-two, even if that does make my sons illegitimate.

❧ NANCY ASTOR

An old woman…is a person who has no sense of decency; if once she takes to living, the devil himself can't get rid of her.

❧ FANNY BURNEY

Age seldom arrives smoothly or quickly. It's more often a succession of jerks.

❧ JEAN RHYS

Lionel Barrymore first played my grandfather, later my father, and finally, he played my husband. If he'd lived, I'm sure I'd have played his mother. That's the way it is in Hollywood. The men get younger and the women get older.

ᴑ LILLIAN GISH

If I had the use of my body I would throw it out of the window.

❧ SAMUEL BECKETT, *MALONE DIES*

I can't actually see myself putting makeup on my face at the age of sixty. But I can see myself going on a camel train to Samarkand.

❧ GLENDA JACKSON

We are all born mad.
Some remain so.

❧ SAMUEL BECKETT, *WAITING FOR GODOT*

We always find
something, eh Didi, to
give us the impression
that we exist?

❧ SAMUEL BECKETT, *WAITING FOR GODOT*

If you think that you have caught a cold, call in a good doctor. Call in three good doctors and play bridge.

❧ ROBERT BENCHLEY

The trouble with life isn't that there is no answer, it's that there are so many answers.

❧ Ruth Benedict

Life is rather like a tin of sardines—we're all of us looking for the key.

❦ ALAN BENNETT

I don't deserve this, but
I have arthritis and I
don't deserve that either.

❧ JACK BENNY (SAID WHEN ACCEPTING AN
AWARD)

Old age is…a lot of crossed off names in an address book.

 RONALD BLYTHE

It ain't over 'til it's over.

֍ YOGI BERRA

INFANCY, n. The period of our lives when, according to Wordsworth, "Heaven lies about us." The world begins lying about us pretty soon afterwards.

  AMBROSE BIERCE, *THE DEVIL'S DICTIONARY*

CHILDHOOD, n. The period of human life intermediate between the idiocy of infancy and the folly of youth—two removes from the sin of manhood and three from the remorse of age.

꙾ AMBROSE BIERCE, *THE DEVIL'S DICTIONARY*

PRESENT, n. That part of eternity dividing the domain of disappointment from the realm of hope.

 AMBROSE BIERCE, *THE DEVIL'S DICTIONARY*

FUTURE, n. That period of time in which our affairs prosper, our friends are true, and our happiness is assured.

    ❧ AMBROSE BIERCE, *THE DEVIL'S DICTIONARY*

LONGEVITY, n. Uncommon extension of the fear of death.

❧ AMBROSE BIERCE, *THE DEVIL'S DICTIONARY*

It's not perfect,
but to me
on balance Right Now
is a lot better than
the Good Old Days.

❧ MAEVE BINCHY